Christmas Primer

A Very Easy Book of Christmas Carols
For Piano or Electronic Keyboard
By Wesley Schaum

Foreword

This book is designed to make familiar Christmas carols as easy as possible. A student with just six to eight weeks study will be able to start enjoying this album.

The pieces are arranged in five-finger position with melody divided between the hands. A minimum of finger numbers is used. Large, widely spaced notes help make music reading easier. Rests have been purposely omitted so the student can focus on the notes.

Duet accompaniments offer many possibilities for recitals and Sunday school participation. The duets help provide rhythmic training and ensemble experience especially valuable to beginners. The person playing the accompaniment is free to add pedal according to his/her own taste.

The duets are recommended for use at home as well as at the lesson. However, the student should work alone at first until the notes and rhythm of the solo part are secure.

Index

EXCLUSIVELY DISTRIBUTED BY
HAL•LEONARD® CORPORATION
7777 W. BLUEMOUND RD. P.O. BOX 13819 MILWAUKEE, WI 53213

© Copyright 1970 by Schaum Publications, Inc., Mequon, Wisconsin • International Copyright Secured • All Rights Reserved • Printed in U.S.A.

ISBN-13: 978-1-936098-35-4

Jolly Old St. Nicholas

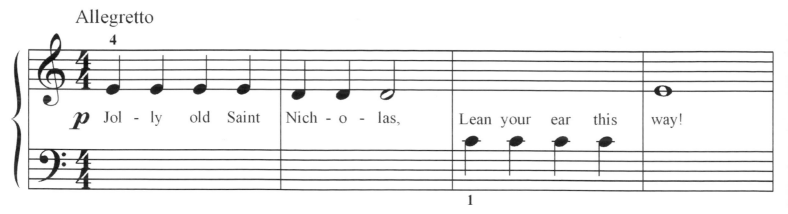

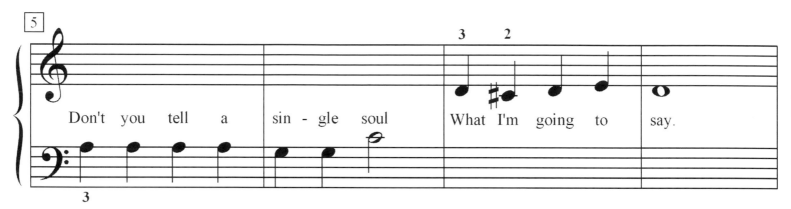

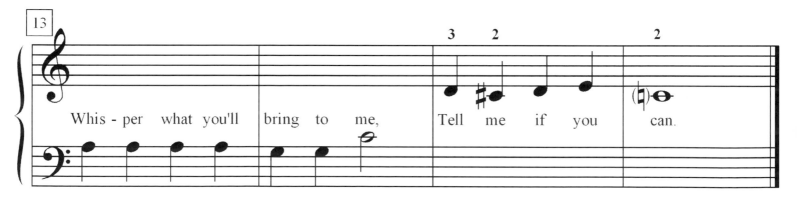

Duet Accompaniment
(Stem up = R.H. Stem down = L.H.)

Toyland

Andantino

mp Toy - land! Toy - land!

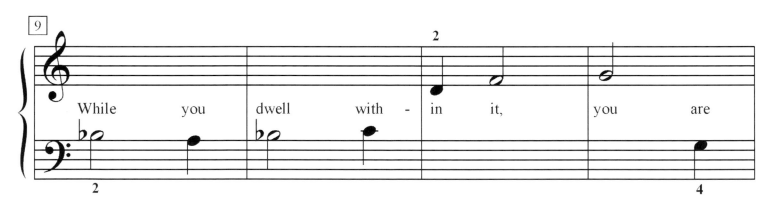

Dear lit - tle girl and boy land.

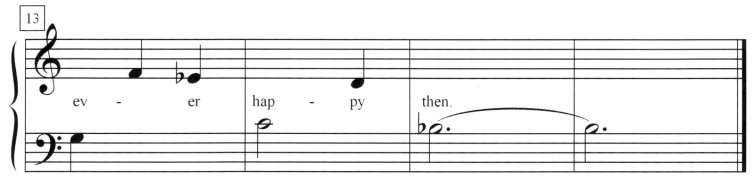

While you dwell with - in it, you are

ev - er hap - py then.

Duet Accompaniment

mp

O Come, All Ye Faithful

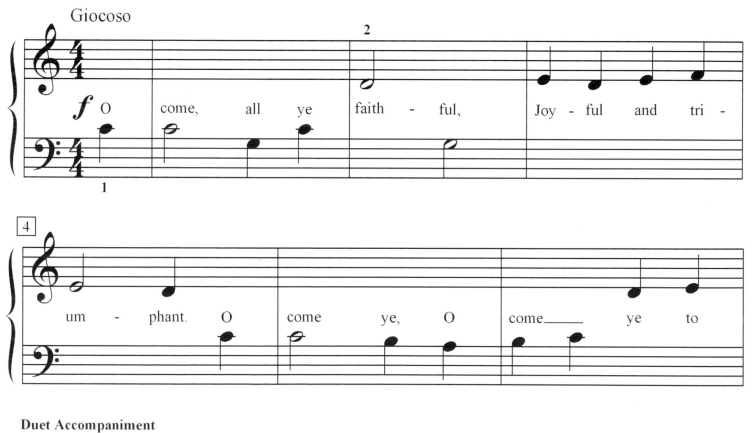

Giocoso

f O come, all ye faith - ful, Joy - ful and tri -

um - phant. O come ye, O come_____ ye to

Duet Accompaniment

f

Teacher's Note: If the pupil is in the early grades in school and has not yet had fractions, do not attempt to explain the dotted quarter-eighth note pattern. The rule to follow is this: *experience should precede explanation.* Teach the rhythm by rote. Delay the explanation until the situation arises at a later time when the student has acquired fraction readiness.

5

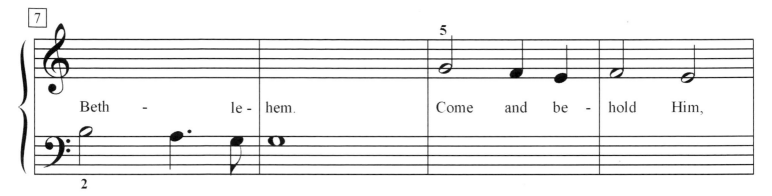

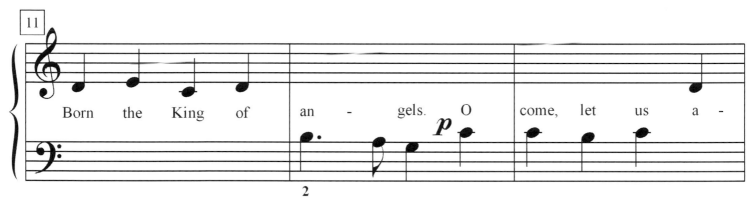

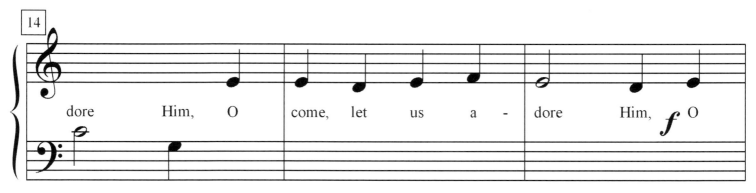

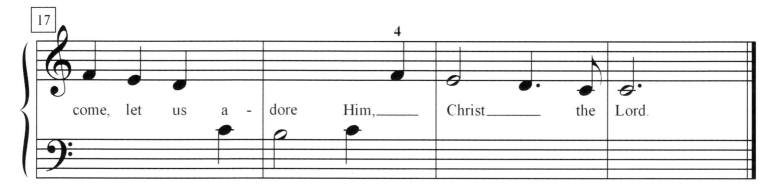

Duet Accompaniment (continued)

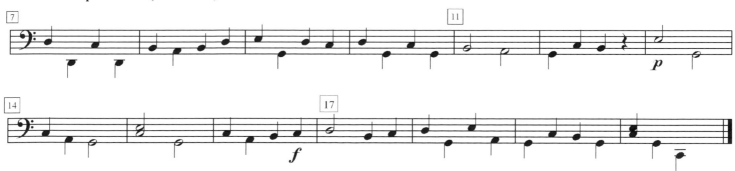

Friendly Beasts

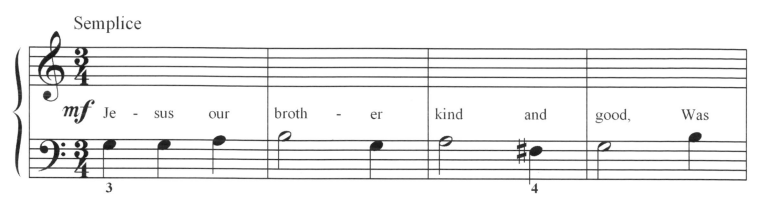

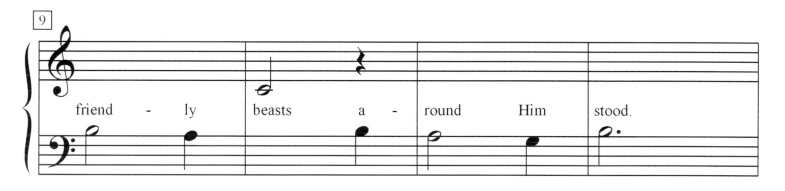

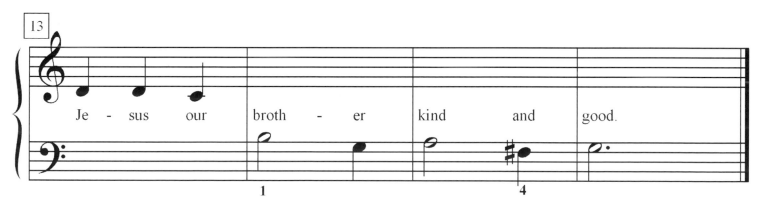

Duet Accompaniment

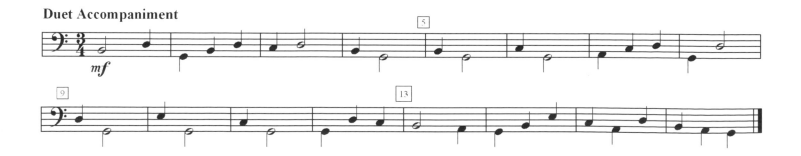

O Come, Little Children

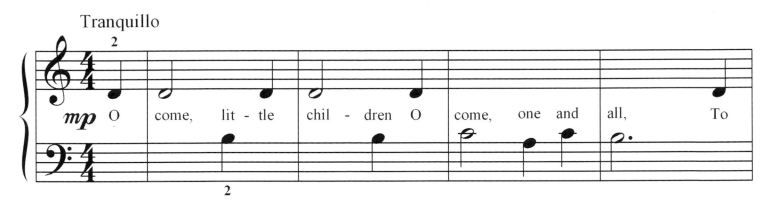

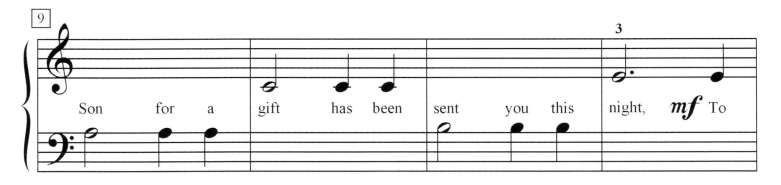

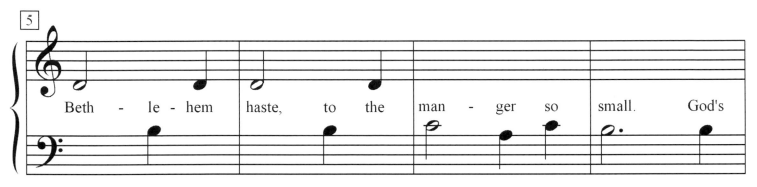

Duet Accompaniment

We Three Kings of Orient Are

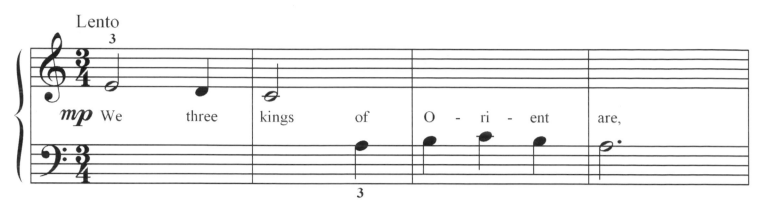

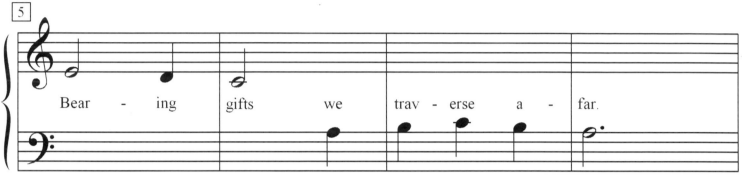

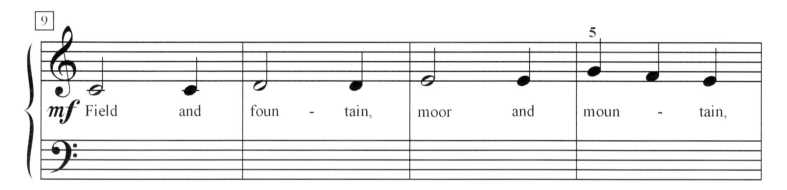

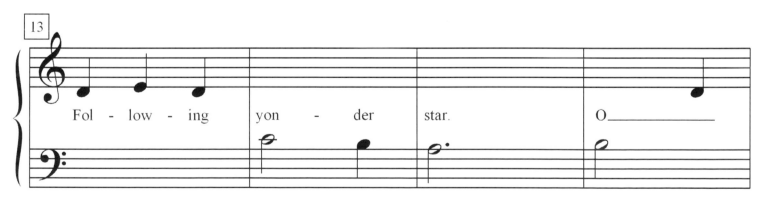

Duet Accompaniment

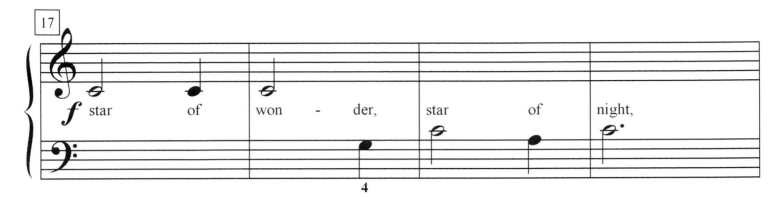

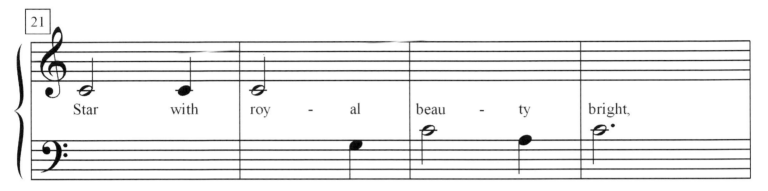

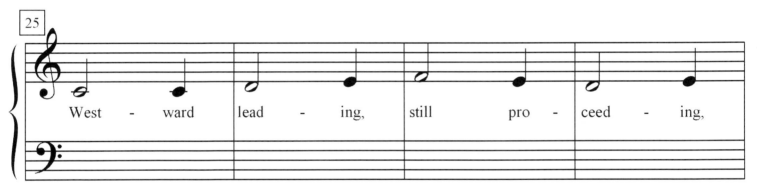

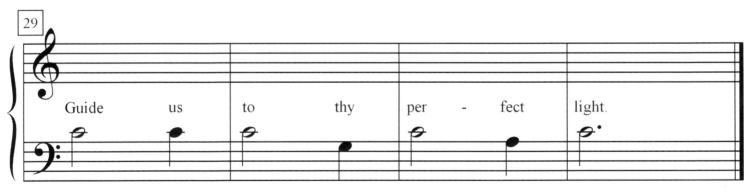

Duet Accompaniment (continued)

O Little Town of Bethlehem

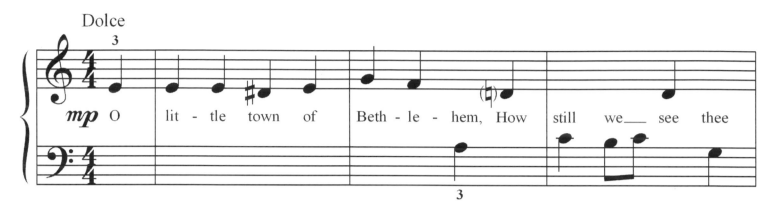

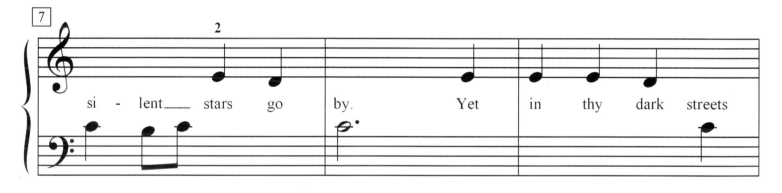

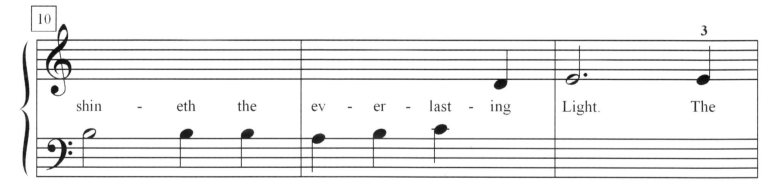

Duet Accompaniment

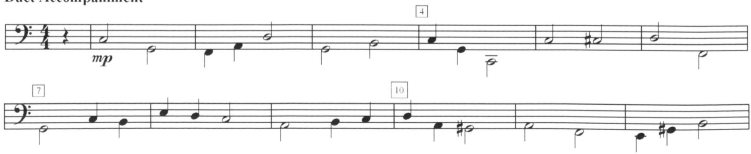

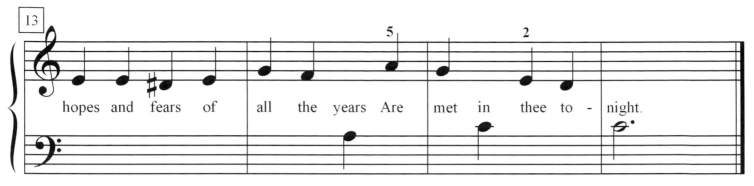

hopes and fears of all the years Are met in thee to - night.

Duet Accompaniment (continued)

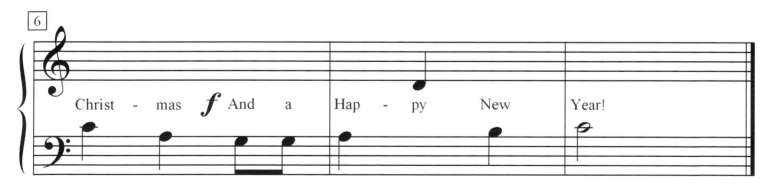

We Wish You a Merry Christmas

Animato

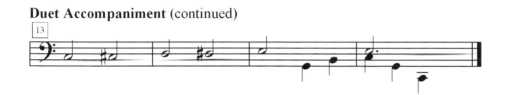

mf We wish you a Mer - ry Christ - mas, We

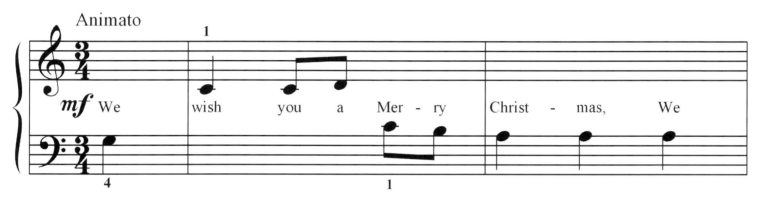

wish you a Mer - ry Christ - mas, We wish you a Mer - ry

Christ - mas *f* And a Hap - py New Year!

Duet Accompaniment

Silent Night

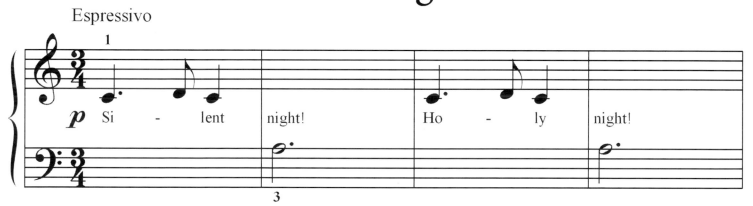

Espressivo

p Si - lent night! Ho - ly night!

All is calm, all is bright,

Duet Accompaniment

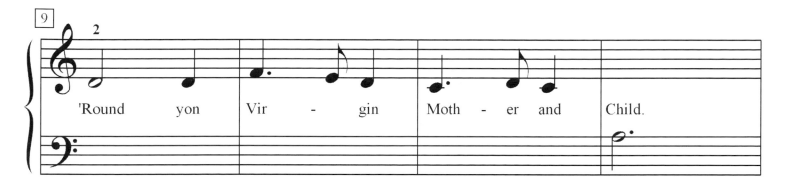

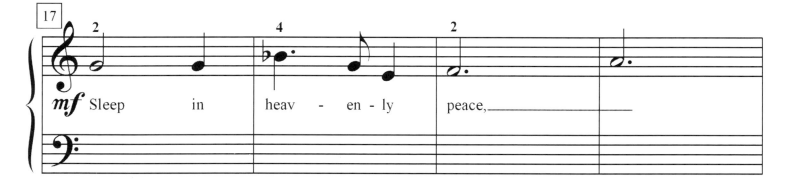

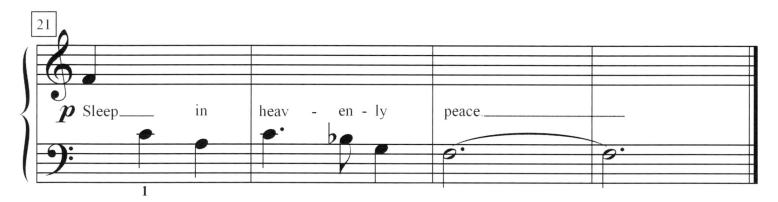

Duet Accompaniment (continued)

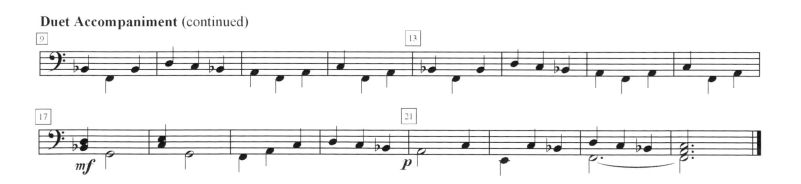

Up on the Housetop

Vivace

mf Up on the house-top the rein - deer pause, Out jumps good old

San - ta Claus. Down through the chim - ney with lots of toys,

Duet Accompaniment

mf

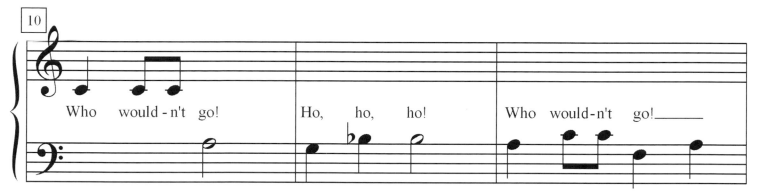

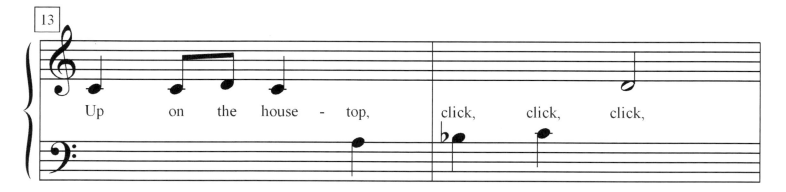

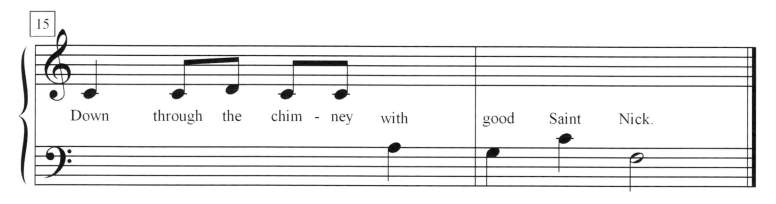

Duet Accompaniment (continued)

Hark the Herald Angels Sing

Maestoso

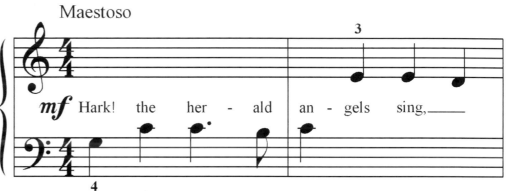

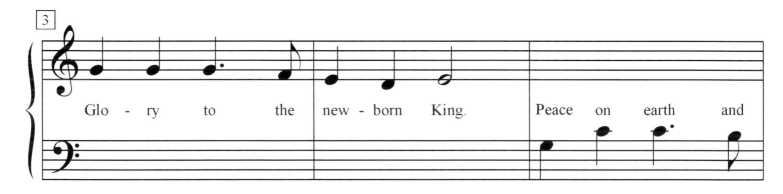

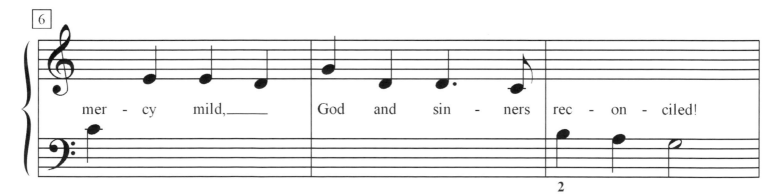

Duet Accompaniment

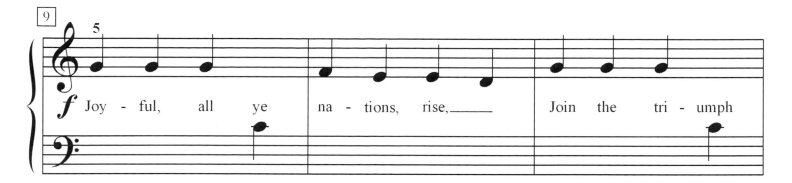

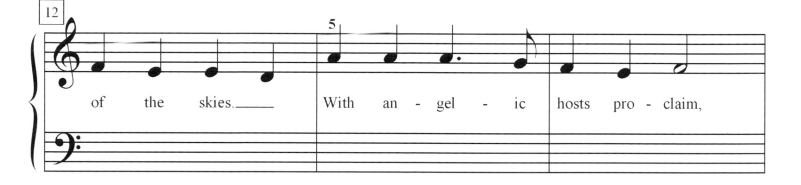

Duet Accompaniment (continued)

Away in a Manger

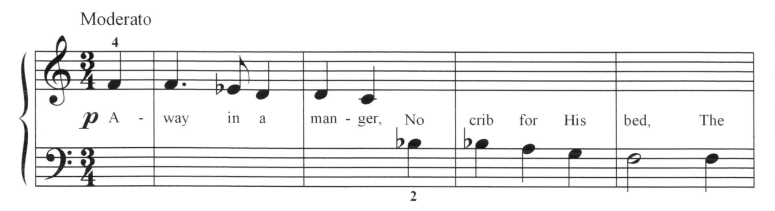

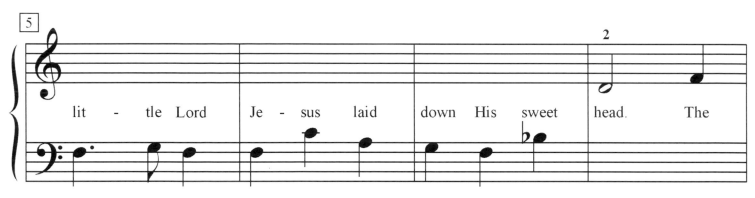

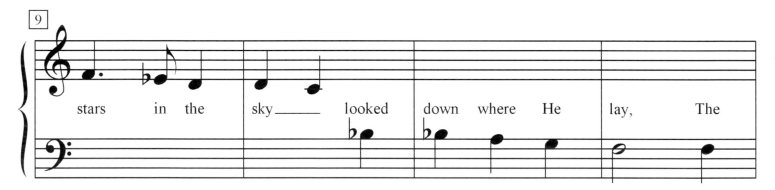

Duet Accompaniment

Jingle Bells

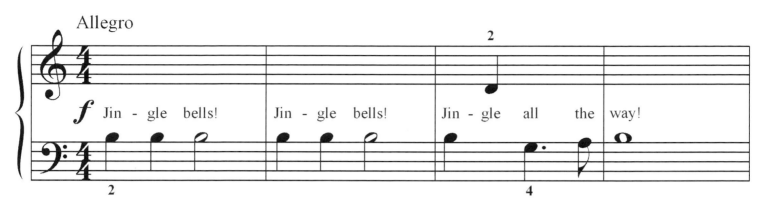

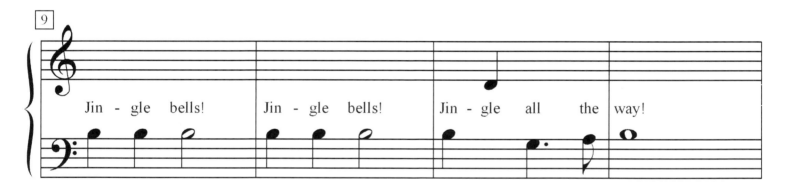

Duet Accompaniment

Joy to the World

Con anima

Joy to the world! The Lord is

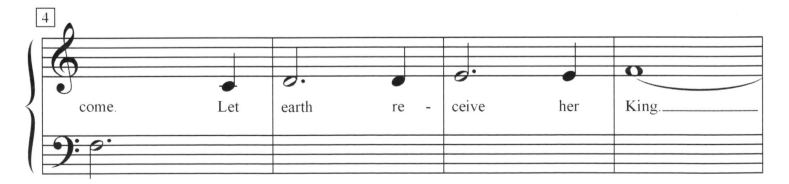

come. Let earth re - ceive her King.

Duet Accompaniment

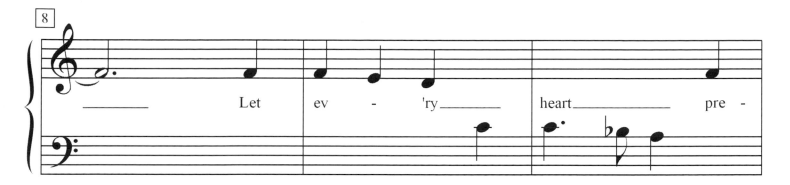

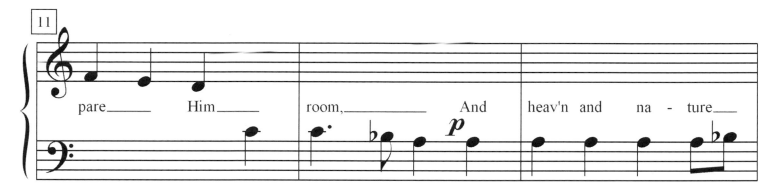

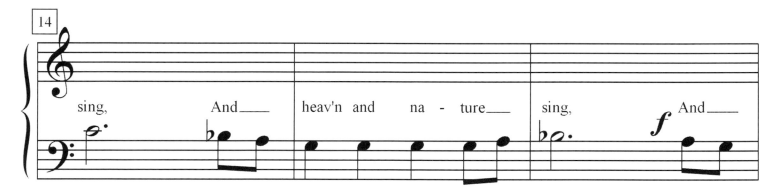

Duet Accompaniment (continued)

The First Noel

Duet Accompaniment

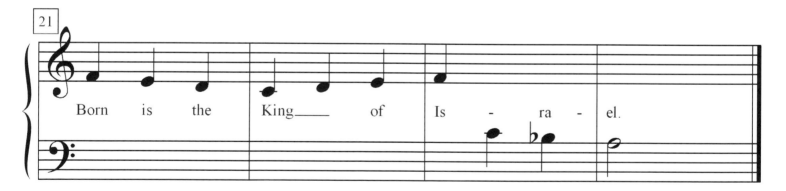

Duet Accompaniment (continued)